The Happy Network Marketer

The Wealthy & Fun Way to Build My Business

KEITH & TOM "BIG AL" SCHREITER

The Happy Network Marketer: The Wealthy & Fun Way to Build My Business

© 2022 by Keith & Tom "Big Al" Schreiter

Published by Fortune Network Publishing

PO Box 890084

Houston, TX 77289 USA

+1 (281) 280-9800

BigAlBooks.com

Print ISBN: 978-1-956171-09-9

Ebook ISBN: 978-1-956171-08-2

Contents

Preface

We know the old saying:

"Mondays don't stink. It is what we do on Mondays that stinks."

So, why not change what we do on Mondays?

The same holds true for network marketing.

"Network marketing isn't hard. It is how we choose to do network marketing that is hard."

So why not make building our business a fun and fantastic experience? Yes, we can build our business within our comfort zones, and enjoy every step along the way.

What happens when we attempt to contact and sell prospects in ways that make us feel bad? Procrastination. No motivation. Feels like hard work. And we don't look forward to building our future in network marketing.

Here is our plan. Don't build our business with uncomfortable activities. Instead, let's take the time to search out activities that work for us. There are so many rejection-free methods we can use. Let's choose the ways that make us smile.

When we look forward to building our business every day, we will love our network marketing careers.

Wealth, freedom, and happiness. Let's learn how.

What do these short stories have in common?

There is the often-told story of the businessman and the fisherman. While there are many variations, it seems that Heinrich Boll wrote the original version. Here is the abbreviated story.

The story tells of a happy fisherman who lived on a beach and enjoyed fishing in the morning. Then he spent the rest of the day enjoying time with his family and friends.

A businessman encouraged the fisherman to spend more time fishing, buy a bigger boat, diversify into processing the fish, build a huge company, take the bigger company to New York and sell its stock publicly and make millions of dollars.

The fisherman asks, "How long will this take?"

The businessman replies, "Ten to fifteen years. And then you can take all those millions to … retire near a beach, fish a little, and enjoy time with your family and friends."

Ouch.

Hate our job?

Comedian Drew Carey said, "Oh, you hate your job? Why didn't you say so? There is a support group for that. It's called EVERYBODY, and they meet at the bar."

Sad. True for many. And this is not the life we want.

Ask ourselves this question, "How many people do we know that hate their jobs? How many people do we know who hate waking up early, leaving their family, and commuting to their hated jobs?"

If we hate our jobs, we are not alone. There are many, many other people like us who want to sleep in on Mondays, and then do what they want to do with their lives.

But this bad job situation won't change if all we do is "wish" for it.

Comedian Ellen Goodman said: "Normal is getting dressed in clothes that you buy for work and driving through traffic in a car that you are still paying for–in order to get to the job you need to pay for the clothes and the car, and the house you leave vacant all day so you can afford to live in it."

Groan.

That quote would be depressing if it wasn't so true.

I wonder if one then needs a part-time job to help pay for the alcohol to continue this grind.

Sometimes our best plans don't work out.

Will an expensive education guarantee wealth?

A university education is great. It can open doors, qualify us for higher paying careers, and we might create a network of classmates for our future network.

Unfortunately, university costs a lot. Some graduates will never get their investment back. They will carry that university debt for the rest of their lives. There are no guarantees in life.

Worse yet, what if we got a philosophy degree, and then found out the philosophy factories weren't hiring?

There is an old joke that goes like this:

Q. What is the reward for graduating from university with an impractical degree?

A. Massive debt and 40 years of hard labor.

One skeptic described getting a university education as, "Paying for school just to get a job … so that the job can pay for school."

Well, it isn't normally that bad, but student loan payments can feel depressing.

So, what do these short stories have in common?

Dissatisfaction.

We want to be wealthy. We want to be happy. But, we need a better plan.

The first step is to know exactly what we want. No one wants to work hard for a goal, and then discover they chose the wrong goal.

Our journey to wealth and happiness is more fun when we know exactly where we are going.

Ready?

What is wealth?

What does wealth mean to us?

- A big monthly income?
- A fancy car to show off to others?
- Respect from our peers?
- All the holidays we can take?
- A 10-bedroom house in a luxury neighborhood?
- A bank account with lots of numbers?
- Connections for front row concert tickets?

Nice things for sure. But wealth? Let's see.

What about money?

Accumulation of money isn't wealth. More digits on our bank account statement mean nothing if we don't have time to celebrate this money. Few people want to work every waking hour of their lives, and then die.

Imagine having an 8-figure savings account at the bank. But, we live on a small tropical island where everyone barters fish, clothing, and housing. Our bank account is useless. Numbers in our bank account don't seem to fit the full definition of wealth. But what else could we consider?

What about more stuff?

How about a fancy car or a big house? Collecting more stuff? Is that wealth? We want others to look at what we have and feel jealous. We want to show off our accomplishments. Let's take some photos of us standing in front of our stuff and post them on social media.

Well, this could bring a smile to our faces briefly. But then, we have to worry and pay and protect and clean and maintain and … well, so much for us to do to "watch our stuff." Watching our stuff is not a fun full-time job.

What about more time?

Billionaires on their deathbed. Will these billionaires trade millions or billions for more time in their lives? Yes!

Whoa! So, what could be more valuable than money and stuff? Time!

More money is great. But the biggest benefit of money? Money gives us more quality time. With enough money, we won't have to sell 40 hours of our time every week to earn a living.

Imagine what happens with more money. We gift ourselves some "time freedom" that we own. We get the freedom to enjoy and pursue our real passions without a 9-to-5 job interfering with our day.

- Don't have to wake up to an alarm in the mornings? Yes, there is freedom in that.
- Don't have to work overtime and weekends to keep our jobs? Yes, there is freedom in that.
- Don't have to take on a part-time job to buy groceries for the family? Yes, there is freedom in that.

More time that we control is closer to true wealth.

What about freedom?

Now we are getting closer to our wealth definition. When we have enough money, and we have some discretionary time that we own, we have the freedom to make choices.

So many people feel frustrated in life. Why? Because they don't have the freedom to choose what to do with their time.

Freedom to choose gives us the feeling of control. We smile because we have the opportunity to design what we do with our waking hours. We can choose to watch television or go on a walk. We can choose to train for a sporting event. We can choose to spend more time with our children.

We like the feeling of freedom.

And that brings us to …

What about … happiness?

A great definition of "wealth" could be … happiness.

Isn't that why we collect things? Want goals? Want freedom?

Yes! Our ultimate goal is to be happy. Happiness = wealth.

How can we define happiness? How about this definition?

"We enjoy exactly what we are doing right now, with our time."

All the money, all the stuff, all the free time, all the freedom choices point towards one goal: "To be happy at this moment."

When we are truly wealthy, we are happy right now. Nothing we could do would feel better than what we experience right now.

Isn't that what we want wealth to be?

This is possible by designing a life we don't need a vacation from. Instead, let's make every day a vacation day, doing what we enjoy.

And now for the good news.

We don't have to wait to accumulate a million dollars in our checking account or even quit our job. Instead, we can design our network marketing business and life into activities that we love. That way every moment we can do exactly what makes us happy.

This isn't a new idea. Here is a old quote attributed to Confucius:

"Choose a job you love, and you will never have to work a day in your life."

Not sure that is exactly what he said, but the advice is great. If we find something we like to do now, and can make it our job, how awesome is that?

Need an example? Golf.

Jerry Scribner loves golfing. He also loves talking to people about his network marketing business. Not hard to see how this will work, right?

On weekdays, when the golf courses are not crowded, Jerry can go to a different golf course daily. Nice. And since he goes alone, the golf course will put him into a foursome with three strangers (prospects). Jerry hacks away at the golf course, enjoys the sport, and has three new "captive" prospects. What do they talk about? Their lives. Their jobs. Their businesses. And most prospects want to know how Jerry can golf every weekday.

Every day is a good day for Jerry and his business. Happiness.

Another golf example?

Hans Parge also loves golf. He says it is a great way for him to meet people while playing 18 holes. For Hans, this gives him time to find out their wants and needs, and if there is an opportunity to be of service. Hans tells us that golfing is a great place to find like-minded people and to build new relationships. While golf doesn't build character in a person, Hans mentions that golf will quickly reveal a person's character. We can imagine Hans grabbing his golf clubs in the morning and saying to his wife, "Honey, I am off prospecting. And if needed, I might have to work overtime."

But not everything is sunshine and golf all the time.

This is what happened to Jerry. A back injury and back surgery meant no more golfing for a while. Does that mean Jerry couldn't build his business in a pleasurable way? No. It only means that Jerry can change to a different activity for prospecting. Might as well pick an activity that he loves.

Eating.

Jerry loves eating out. He has his favorite morning restaurant that is busy with salesmen and business people. Great prospects for conversation. Jerry and his wife eat out for lunch and dinner every chance they get. Since Jerry is an outgoing blue personality, he meets and strikes up conversations with fellow diners, the restaurant staff, and anyone nearby.

But Jerry also loves playing guitar. Twenty-plus years ago, Jerry's band was nominated for a Grammy. He couldn't pursue his music then, but now with network marketing, he can reactivate his music passion. Guess what Jerry does on weekends? Jams with other bluegrass musicians. Now Jerry can afford his dream camps and meets other musicians around the country. And yes, his new acquaintances all want to know how Jerry can afford his music passion.

But we may be thinking, "Well, that is okay for Jerry. He knows what to say. He loves talking to strangers. But … but … what about me? I don't know how to even start? Everything is uncomfortable for me!"

Good point. Jerry already found his happiness methods for prospecting.

The lesson is clear.

We need to find our freedom and happiness.

Life is too short to spend our week working a job that we hate.

Low motivation and procrastination magically goes away when we love what we do.

Let's take a look at one more version, and then we will learn how to make this happen for us.

Wealth/Happiness formula at work.

Our friend, Steve Porter, is a trial lawyer and a part-time network marketer.

Here is how he designed his Wealth/Happiness formula. We could call it the "What is new with you?" formula.

First, Steve decided the size of the bonus check did not dictate the happiness in his life. After all, a trial lawyer earns much more than minimum wage. But what was more important for Steve?

His daily method of operation. Making cold calls or doing uncomfortable prospecting techniques didn't appeal to Steve. He thought, "If I am going to do network marketing, I want to enjoy it now. I don't want to do unpleasant tasks for months or years in the hopes of a payoff in the future. Life is too short to not be happy now."

Steve's plan? Focus on a simple daily activity or routine that he enjoyed. Here are two examples.

#1. In-person. Steve starts his conversation with, "I'm just curious, what's new with you"? These words and the conversation that follows created "instant rapport" between Steve and his new acquaintance. His goal is not to look for prospects. His goal is to make some new acquaintances. Then, he sees where the conversation takes them.

What happens? The new acquaintances love talking about what is new with them. Many of them reciprocate and ask Steve, "And, what is new with you?"

Steve's answer depends on the conversation so far, but many times it immediately leads to a "two-minute story" presentation. For example, he sometimes replies with, "Thank you for asking! What's new with me is that I have a good story! Takes about two minutes! Might make you a lot of money, might not! Want to hear it?"

#2. Online prospecting. Steve loves this low-key approach to expand his acquaintances. He consistently reaches out to 10 strangers a day on social media. Works for him. Why? Because Steve mastered the art of "instant rapport" with people. This common-sense skill immediately gets them to talk about what we have in common. This overcomes the mistrust strangers have in talking with us.

Again, Steve takes the volunteers. Life is too short for conflict and stress. He reports that now, "I will never run out of people to create relationships with."

Steve's basic tools are these three key magic phrases:

1. "I'm just curious …"
2. "I just found out …"
3. "Would it be okay if …"

He reports that these three key magic phrases turned him into a contacting machine with no more fears!

The big picture plan for Steve? Meet new people and take the volunteers.

But this is so low-key. How does Steve close his prospects?

This is exactly what he says. Ready?

"It's okay to do nothing and keep your life as it is! Or, you can learn some new skills and change your life for the better, like my team and I did! The choice is up to you! I just wanted to give you one more option in your life!"

Done.

His prospects now have a choice.

What a great way to tell prospects to join, or not. We love how polite Steve is with all of his new friends.

The verdict?

These daily activities are fun. Every minute of Steve's network marketing career focuses on what Steve enjoys. Sort of describes happiness, right?

Steve posts often in our study group. This post describes what happens with his friendly approach and follow-ups.

• • •

"When do you stop following up with your network marketing prospects? Never, unless they ask you to stop!

"I first met a guy from Georgia online in 2017 when he 'liked' one of my Facebook ads!

"Now over two years later he is coming to work with my team in my network marketing business! Why?

"Because I never stopped following up with him!"

• • •

Curious about how Steve follows up with his prospects? In his own words, "I love following up with people by sending them narrative text messages describing what I am doing!"

Steve understands the value of telling stories to bypass the salesman alarm in our prospects' minds. This gives us the chance to talk directly to the decision-making part of the brain.

That's it. Easy.

Okay, Steve does his business differently than Jerry. We see there is more than one way to do our business. Finding our way can make the difference between forcing ourselves to build our business ... and having fun and looking forward to building our business.

We want to enjoy every minute of our business activities.

Feeling the magic?

Talking to people, even strangers, can now be stress-free and rejection-free.

1. Start with, "What is new with you?" Allow our prospects to talk about their favorite subject, themselves. Instant rapport and trust.

2. Usually our prospects reciprocate by asking us, "What is new with you?" This gives us permission to introduce what we want to into the conversation.

Now we have permission to introduce our "ice breaker" into the conversation.

Uh-oh.

We don't have a good ice breaker? We don't know what to say next? We are afraid of looking like a salesman? We want to avoid rejection?

Then now is the time to fix this problem. Let's learn how to introduce our business into a social conversation.

The horrible,
untold secret.

Most advice on building our business comes with one ugly flaw.

Flaw: The advice worked for the person who is giving the advice.

We are not that person. Our circumstances are different, our personalities are different, our risk tolerances are different, and our previous life skills are definitely different.

There are many ways to build in network marketing. Not just one way. We should look for methods that are comfortable for us. Then, every day will be a pleasant experience.

- We won't need iron-fisted willpower to force ourselves to do distasteful prospecting methods.

- We won't have to be a schedule-Nazi and have every 15 minutes of our life preplanned.

- We won't have to motivate ourselves as we will enjoy what we do.

Ah, the benefit of comfortable.

So many benefits. Let's make this happen.

The quickest, shortest, and easiest way to kickstart our business.

What do we do in network marketing?

1. We talk to prospects.
2. We gift them an additional option for their lives.
3. We take "yes" decisions from the volunteers who want what we have to offer.

Pretty simple, right?

Except for the details.

- How do we do this?
- How do we do this without rejection?
- How can we be comfortable with the process?

No one wants to feel "icky" for the rest of their life approaching people with sleazy sales tactics.

Then, how do we start before we master better skills?

By concentrating on basics that will make the most difference in our results.

What happens when we talk to our prospects?

They decide if what we offer is good for them or not. And, they will do this quickly.

Here are the four steps they process in their minds.

Step #1: (Rapport) Do I know you? Can I trust you? Can I believe you?

Step #2: (Ice Breaker) So what is this all about?

Step #3: (Closing) Do I want this or not?

Step #4: (Presentation) Give me the details.

That is it! Short and simple.

But wait! Aren't these steps out of order?

No.

This is how human minds process decisions. Here is an example.

We are at our child's boring recital. All of the parents yawn while waiting for their child's turn.

Step #1: Rapport. Automatic. We have a common bond with the other suffering parents.

Step #2: Our ice breaker. Here is our offer to the other parents.

We stand up and announce, "I am taking my child out for ice cream and video games. Who wants to come with us?"

Half the parents say, "Yes!"

Half the parents say "no" to our offer. They have obligations at home, they are lactose intolerant, or on a diet.

Done.

We announced our ice breaker offer and ...

Step #3: The parents made an immediate "yes" or "no" decision before we made our big presentation or told them to watch our ice cream video. Humans make decisions instantly, before the information.

Step #4: The information. The details. Only the parents who want to join us will want the details. These parents are pre-sold. They want the address of the ice cream parlor, and want to know who is going to pay.

Okay. Let's not fill this book with more obvious examples. But to review, this is what happens in our prospects' minds.

Step #1: I know you. I can trust you.

Step #2: We deliver our ice breaker offer.

Step #2: Our prospects make a decision if this is for them or not.

Step #4: If they say "yes" to our ice breaker offer, then we deliver the details.

The old-world method of subjecting prospects to an hour of information and facts before asking for a decision doesn't work. It violates how humans want to make decisions.

Humans want to make instant decisions to save time. And then, if their decision is "yes" … they will want the details.

Make our conversations safe and fun.

Why did I fire my sadistic personal trainer?

The short story?

If we don't enjoy the process, we quit.

My body is a donut storage warehouse, not a lean, mean, exercise machine. But, in a rare moment of mental weakness, I decided to look better and be healthier. So, I took action and hired a professional personal trainer.

What happened?

The first day of training started with a one mile jog on a treadmill. The only thing I ever jogged was my memory. Twelve agonizing minutes later, the one-mile death jog was over.

Exhausted. Out of breath. I think, "My first day of getting into shape will be my last day of getting into shape. Pain hurts."

But then, my over-fit sadistic personal trainer announces, "Now that you finished the warm-up, it is time to start your training exercises."

Not funny. She is now unemployed.

A one mile jog is warming up her muscles. That is where she is on the ladder of physical fitness. That is not where I am.

It is the same with the prospects we talk to while building our network marketing business. In the four steps of our prospecting encounters, rapport is the first step. We have to meet people where they are, not where we are.

We may have the vision of an entrepreneur, we may have a good self-image, and we may be motivated to excel. But are our prospects? Maybe our prospects are not at the same level of vision and achievement that we are. We attended more motivational meetings and read more inspiring books.

Our prospects see the world differently than we do. Our business conversations must be from our prospects' viewpoint, not ours. If not, our prospects "fire us" and stop listening.

The first step is always rapport.

If we have rapport, then we can begin our presentation. If we don't have rapport, then we will have objections and resistance.

New distributors always skip the rapport step. They don't know how to create instant rapport with their prospects. They need to learn quickly. That is our job as sponsors.

A good word to remember? Empathy.

That is a great start in building rapport.

Now our conversations feel pleasant and not stressed. We will look forward to talking with others to share our message.

Rapport first, and then our ice breaker that presents our offer. Good manners.

But we want the shortcut, right?

We want to start immediately and get results. The secret shortcut?

Use a great ice breaker that introduces what we have to offer.

If we can create an awesome one or two-sentence ice breaker that describes what we offer, our prospects will instantly react. They will make their "yes" or "no" decision before we get to the next sentence. Seems magical, but this shortcut rocks!

Before we create a great magic formula for ice breakers, let's look at why this shortcut works.

Here is a graphic that shows how important each of the four steps are when talking to prospects.

Of course, these numbers are approximate, but

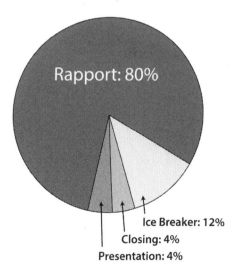

Rapport: 80%

Ice Breaker: 12%
Closing: 4%
Presentation: 4%

we see which of the four steps are more important. Rapport and our ice breaker represent over 90% of our success!

Another shortcut tip.

When we start our network marketing business, we don't have much skill. However, do we notice how other networkers have instant success with their friends and family? Why?

Because they have rapport. Their prospects know them. They don't have to do the 80% of the work. They already built rapport. This explains why talking to strangers is so hard. Strangers may not trust us or believe us. But friends and family? They know us. We have rapport.

If we talk to our warm market, to people who know us, most times we can skip the rapport step. This makes it easy for new team members.

But what is the second most important step? The ice breaker!

This is where we introduce our business into a social conversation. When we introduce what we offer, our prospects will make an immediate "yes" or "no" knee-jerk decision if they are interested or not. If we get this right, this shortcut will make us better than 90% of our competition.

The closing happens automatically at that moment. The presentation details are minor.

The big, scary event that we need to master?

The ice breaker.

Our ice breaker must be so good that prospects think, "I want this. Okay, I will give up units of my life (time) to know more."

In the next chapter, we will look at the ultimate ice breaker formula that works for even the shy, inexperienced, socially awkward network marketer. This is the easy secret to starting fast.

But first ...

Let's take a deep breath before taking this advice.

See if this internal conversation seems familiar.

Us: "I want to build my network marketing business. I can dream of big things and a better life."

Brain: "You don't talk to anyone. This isn't going to happen."

Us: "Well, I haven't talked to anyone after those first few rejections. Plus, I feel a bit awkward asking my friends and family to give me money or to join."

Brain: "Go watch television. We don't want to feel embarrassed."

Us: "But I want this business to work so much!"

Brain: "Wanting is different from doing. You are not doing anything. You are not talking to prospects. Go watch cats playing with string on social media."

Us: "But ... but ... I just don't feel comfortable approaching or talking to prospects."

Brain: "Then stop whining and fix it. Learn exactly what to say and do in a way that feels comfortable. Others have done this. You can too."

Us: "But … but … others are smarter than me. And better looking too."

Brain: "Good point. But you can choose to learn the simple skills to do this, even with your limited abilities."

Us: "But … but … I just don't know how to feel comfortable when approaching or talking to people. Maybe I should listen to that obnoxious motivational speaker who preached:

- "Just do it!"
- "Face the fear!"
- "Eye of the tiger!"
- "Take no prisoners!"
- "Cowards don't win battles!"
- "Be brave!"
- "Don't hold back!"
- "Ignore the fear!"
- "Barge ahead!"
- "No regrets!"
- "Only losers have feelings!"
- "Crush the prospects!"
- "This war!"

Brain: "So we should move blindly forward with passion?"

Us: "Whoops. That sounds scary. How many fearless people do we know?"

Brain: "Not many. Most of the fearless people we know died because they didn't listen to their fears."

Us: "Gulp! So why are we feeling these scary vibes?"

Brain: "Because fear has a place in our lives. Our fear is telling us, 'Careful. Stop doing stupid, dangerous stuff.'"

Us: "So maybe fear is not something to be afraid of. We should consider fear as an early warning system to make sure we make better decisions. But … but … how do we do this?"

Brain: "Read the next chapter."

The "ice breaker" formula anyone can use.

We wrote an entire book on ice breakers. We wrote an entire book of great first sentences that connect with prospects. We even wrote a book on how to do our network marketing business in 15 minutes a day.

There are so many ice breakers we can use, so many formulas, and they all work!

But, not every formula will work for us. Why?

We have different backgrounds, different confidence levels, different skill levels and most importantly, we have different comfort levels about which techniques we are willing to do.

How many ice breaker formulas and techniques are there? Hundreds. And they all work for someone.

But ... what is the most universal, easiest, safest, and socially acceptable ice breaker?

Okay, this won't be the most powerful, but anyone can do this secret ice breaker formula from the moment they join. And they will love it.

Let's explain how this works with a Venn diagram.

Using a Venn diagram helps us choose which techniques to use.

Let's look at ice breakers in our social lives. We can think of all the possible ice breakers as a large circle. Some are easy to do while others are difficult. Some cause us to feel awkward, while others feel natural. We call this circle "What Works."

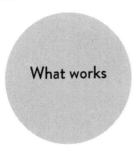

This circle represents the different ice breaker formulas and techniques that work. Imagine there are 1,000 different ice breaker techniques in this circle. Some are hard to use. Some require great skills. Some are easy. But all can work if we have the skill to do them.

The second circle of our Venn diagram?

"My Skills."

This circle represents all the skills we currently have. Yes, if we have more skills, we can use more of the ice breaker formulas and techniques in the first circle.

Now, imagine we are new to network marketing. Our skills are … close to zero. That means we can only use a few of the ice breaker formulas and techniques in the first circle. Yes, our lack of skills limits our choices.

So let's overlap these two circles. As we see, the "My Skills" circle overlaps only a small portion of the "What Works" circle. This represents what we can use now with our limited skills. Let's imagine that we now only have ten ice breaker techniques that we can use now.

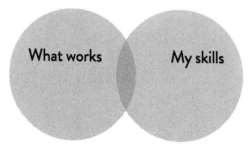

But … we have one more important limiting factor. This one is the most important!

Our comfort zone.

With the ten ice breaker techniques that we know how to use, maybe nine of those techniques make us uncomfortable. Ouch!

If we are uncomfortable with a technique, we feel unhappy. No one wants a career where we hate what we do. And we will stop!

So when we overlap the "My Comfort Zone" circle, what do we see?

A very, very limited choice of ice breaker formulas and techniques that we will find comfortable to use.

And this explains a lot!

Now we understand what holds us back. If we are uncomfortable, if we don't feel safe, we won't use the chosen ice breaker formula or technique.

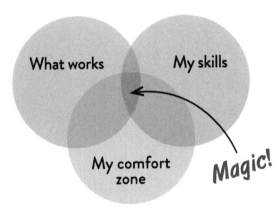

Reaching outside of our comfort zone sounds great in theory. Unfortunately, this is stressful. Our minds find excuses to stay where we are.

Picking an authentic technique within our comfort zone means we won't have to fight our minds every step of the way. Whew! That feels so good.

This isn't about judging what works. This is about judging what we will enjoy using over and over again in real life.

If we love the ice breaker technique we use, we will love our careers.

And here is an extra benefit. Our comfort zone expands every time we use a technique that feels good.

The "ice breaker" formula anyone can use.

Ready?

Step #1: Find a benefit that we love about our business. We love talking about our benefits. Finding benefits is easy. They are everywhere! We hear them all the time from our fellow networkers. Let's make a small list now of business benefits. Of course, we will also create a list of product and service benefits too.

- Work from home.
- Fire the boss.
- More time with the children.
- Two paychecks instead of one paycheck.
- Give ourselves a raise.
- No more commuting.

This is an easy exercise. So many benefits we can list.

Step #2: Ask permission. This is what makes this ice breaker technique comfortable to use. This is the magic in this formula.

Benefit + Permission = Comfortable

Let's put this formula to use. Here are some examples of announcing a benefit, and then asking permission if our prospects want to know more.

First, let's establish a good rapport. Give our prospects a chance to talk first. Encourage them to talk about something that added value to their lives or some new development.

Us: "What is new with you?"

Prospect talks and then asks us: "What is new with you?"

We have rapport. We are in conversation. We politely listened to our prospect. And now our prospect asks us, "What is new with you?"

Time for our ice breaker answer. We will answer with:

Step #1: (benefit)"Looks like I can quit my job at the end of the year."

Step #2: (permission) "Would you like to know how I am going to do it?"

Done.

Instant decision from our prospect. Too easy. Too comfortable. And very effective. In a few seconds, our prospect can decide if our benefit is interesting or not.

How about more examples?

Us: "I will get a small raise every month. Would you like to know how that works?"

Us: "I won't have to commute to work ever again. Would you like to know my secret plan?"

Us: "My neighbor works out of his home full-time now. Would you like to know how he does it?"

Us: "I got a plan so that I will have three-day weekends forever. Would you like to know my plan?"

Us: "I got two Christmas bonuses this year. Would you like to know what happened?"

Us: "My wife now earns more money part-time than her boss does full-time. Would you like to know how she does it?"

Us: "I got a secret plan to escape from this job. Would you like to hear my plan during coffee break?"

Our prospects respond, "Tell me more." We made this easy for them to say "yes" and to ask more about our benefit.

What happens if our prospects are not interested?

They can change the subject and talk about the weather, sports or shopping. This is what happens in all conversations. We change topics often.

But what about my products or services?

Okay. Let's do a few examples to get our imaginations working. This is fun!

Us: "I finally lost those last 20 pounds. Would you like to know what made this happen?"

Us: "I now have more energy than a giant pot of coffee. Would you like to know my new secret?"

Us: "My skin is getting younger now, instead of older. Would you like to know how this is possible?"

Us: "I got rid of all the chemicals in my home. Would you like to know what I am using now?"

Us: "My mobile phone bill is now $30 lower a month. Would you like to know what happened?"

Us: "I found out how to get a discount on our electricity bills. Would you like to know what I found out?"

Us: "My sister showed me how to take five-star holidays for budget prices. Would you like to know what she showed me?

Us: "I decided to live a lot longer. Would you like to know my plan?"

Us: "I am sleeping so much better now. Want to know my secret?"

Enough examples for now. Let's review.

Remember our explanation of what we do in network marketing?

A. We talk to prospects.

B. We give them one more option for their lives.

C. We take "yes" decisions from the volunteers who want what we have to offer.

Now we can introduce our business to others in a way that:

#1: Works.

#2: Is within our skills.

#3: And is polite and comfortable.

We only talk further with those prospects who volunteer and say, "Please tell me more. I am interested in this great benefit."

And now the mystery is solved.

For years, network marketing leaders wondered:

"My team knows exactly what to say. They know exactly what to do. I trained them with the best skills. So why won't they 'pull the trigger' and start prospecting?"

The answer is obvious. The third circle.

If the activity is not within our comfort zone, we won't do it. The third circle is what makes our business a nightmare, or the most fun activity in the world.

If we have team members who hesitate to take action, our job is to find what works, within their skill set, and to make sure it is within their comfort zone.

But, but, but ... one more excuse.

"I don't know what to say within my comfort zone. My sponsor won't help me. I am helpless. I don't know what I don't know!"

True. It is not our fault if we don't know what to say.

But it is our fault if we choose not to learn what to say.

Ouch!

Our icebreaker should feel like play, not like work. Why? Because play doesn't need motivation. We love to play.

If we don't have a comfortable ice breaker now, where can we learn more options?

- A good mentor.
- Millions of Internet pages.
- Trial and error experience.
- On-the-job training with our sponsor.

- Books.
- Audio training.
- Seminars and workshops.
- Common sense.

We either commit to learning how to do our business, or we commit to staying stuck where we are. The decision is up to us.

If we are not comfortable approaching people with our ice breaker, then, why not fix that now?

Fear rejection?

Not anymore. Why?

Because we won't cause rejection. We just learned how to introduce our business into any conversation without offending or pressuring prospects.

Here is the process again:

A. We talk to prospects.

B. We give them one more option for their lives.

C. We take "yes" decisions from the volunteers who want what we have to offer.

The volunteers will ask us to continue this conversation direction. They say, "Oh, tell me more." Or, "How does that work?"

What if our prospects change the subject or don't continue this direction of our conversation? They are telling us "no" or "not right now." Some of their reasons could include:

- They don't want what we offer.
- Someone scratched their car earlier in the day.
- Their favorite sports team lost.
- They don't feel comfortable with us.
- They have stomach cramps from too many donuts.

Notice how these reasons are "all about them" and not about us or our business? People worry about their feelings and their lives. They don't worry about us.

Our job is just letting people know they have options. It is up to them to improve their lives with their choices.

There is no rejection. This isn't personal about us. It is personal about them. They worry about their lives.

How can we adjust our mindsets from selling to gifting an option?

Are there little messages we can tell ourselves to put us into the proper mindsets? Of course. Ready?

- This will either be a good idea for you, or not.
- It is okay to say "no" to my offer. It is entirely up to you.
- You can make it decision to start today. Or, you could make a decision not to start today, and keep your life exactly like it is.
- They don't struggle with my offer. But, they might struggle if now is the time to start changing their lives, or not.
- They may want to move forward, but they may have sub-conscious mind programs to delay and put off change.
- I can only control my activity. I can't control other people.

These thoughts change our intention from "selling" to "gifting options" to prospects. They feel our sincerity and relax. We now remove those negative rejection programs from our prospects' minds.

Don't be like our friend, Earl. His high-agenda motto?

The Happy Network Marketer

"Life is short. I want to make sure I spend as much time as possible on social media arguing with strangers"

Out of our control.

Want to be unhappy? Focus on things outside of our control. That is a recipe for frustration. We don't want to spend time on:

- Reliving what happened in the past.
- What others think about us.
- Trying to control the outcome of our activities.
- What other people decide to do.
- Events that no one can control.
- Opinions of the our friends.

Want to feel happy? Put our energy into what we can control. Then, accept that we did our part.

I got "ghosted" again!

Why do prospects ghost us?

Because they are afraid to say "no" and feel we would try to sell them harder. Or, if we are close friends, they don't want to say "no" to us and ruin our relationship. Again, this is not personal. They don't want the benefit we mentioned now.

"Being ghosted" is not a paranormal experience. "Being ghosted" is our prospects telling us they are not interested now.

The good news?

If these prospects don't want the benefit we offered, this gives us more time to talk with others. Life is easy when we spend our time with eager, ready-to-take-action prospects who want what we offer.

Should we feel rejected when prospects don't show up for an appointment? No. Again, they made a "no" decision and feel embarrassed to tell us. It is okay for others not to take the options we give them. It is okay for them to keep their lives the same. Their choice.

We are not responsible for other people's lives. We are not responsible for the spouse they chose, the sports team they cheer for, how often they clean their living room ... and we are not responsible if they don't want our benefit at this moment.

But what about close friends or prospects who intimidate us?

We don't want people to feel obligated or pressured. Plus, we may be shy about bringing up our business. If this happens, let's fix this stress inside of our minds. How?

These two sentences.

- "I am perfectly comfortable with your decision to look at my business or not."
- "But I was uncomfortable not asking if you wanted to look, and having you think that I didn't care."

The first sentence tells our prospects that we are offering one more option for their lives. It is okay if this option isn't for them. They don't need an excuse to change the subject. No pressure.

The second sentence makes us feel good because this gives us a reason to be in this conversation. We don't want them to feel we would keep a secret from them. Plus, they feel honored that we care.

Our prospects can politely say "no" to us by replying, "Thank you for caring. I don't have an interest now, but appreciate that you thought of us."

No rejection.

Why? Because we make the conversation comfortable for our prospects. They can gracefully move on and change the subject without guilt.

Remember, we only want the volunteers who want our benefits at this time in their lives.

Hate selling?
Then do this.

Make it easy for prospects to say "yes" to our offer.

Let's make this simple. What if we could summarize our offer in one sentence? Then, make sure our sentence was easy to say "yes" to. Now our prospects will sell themselves. Examples?

- Is now a good time to stop paying those higher rates?
- Want to live longer?
- Should we start our freedom plan now, or just give up on the idea?
- Want to lose weight and not be hungry?
- Want to delay wrinkling an extra 8 years?
- Do we want to be in charge of our life?
- Want to help the environment?
- Want to work from your home instead of commuting?

What is standing in our way? We may not have an opening line we are comfortable with … yet. But, now we know what to look for. A simple, one-sentence question that is comfortable for us.

Why does this work so well with prospects? Because people hate to be sold, but love to buy. This gives them control of their choices. We don't have to sell them. We just give them an easy way to say "yes" to our question.

Questions.

Welcome to the magic of using questions to talk to our prospects. Questions don't feel like selling or closing. Questions feel natural as our prospects engage with their answers. Once we are clear about what we offer, this gets easy. Ask questions that lead prospects to see the value in our offers.

Jerry Scribner was enjoying a nice dinner with his wife and two adult daughters at a local restaurant. When dinner finished, three friends came to pick up Jerry's daughters. Since Jerry sells discounted cell phone service, here was the conversation.

Jerry asked his daughters' friends, "Do you know anyone who doesn't have a cell phone?"

All three friends said, "No."

Jerry then asked, "Do you think most people would prefer to pay more or less every month?"

All three friends said, "Less."

This easy conversation continued.

"If you showed your friends how to pay less, would they be happy and thank you?"

All three friends said, "Yes."

"Would it make you feel good to help people?"

All three friends said, "Yes."

Jerry finished the offer by saying, "When your friends pay that bill every month, would it be okay if we sent you a referral payment every month?"

All three friends said, "Yes."

Does this conversation make Jerry happy? Yes. Can we do this? Yes. When we make it easy for prospects to say "yes" to our offers, we will never fear selling again.

But, would this work for health products?

We can modify these five basic questions for anything. This is the short opportunity explanation most prospects would love to hear. So, let's revise these five questions for a health products example.

"Do you know anyone who wants to lose weight or feel younger?"

"Do you think most people would prefer to look and be healthy?"

"If you showed your friends how to look and be healthy, would they be happy and thank you?"

"Would it make you feel good to help people?"

"When your friends lose their weight and get healthy, would it be okay if we gave you some extra money every month for helping them?"

Prospects love it when we explain our business and get to the point without a lot of wasted time.

What if our prospects were pre-sold?

Well, our prospects won't pre-sell themselves unless we help. We can change the entire conversation from "selling" to "helping." How do we do this?

By telling our prospects that they are already sold! Yes, when appropriate, we can tell our prospects they will buy or join anyway. And, we are here to help them make that process easier.

Here are some examples to get us thinking.

- "I don't have to sell you a car because you already know you need to get a car. But, I can help you choose the right car so you make the best choice for your family.

- "I don't have to sell you good health because you know you want to live longer instead of dying quickly. But, I can recommend some ways and supplements to help you."

- "I don't have to sell you on a lower phone bill because you and I both can do third-grade math. We know paying less is smarter."

- "I don't have to convince you to join because you want to have more money without getting another job. I am here to help you kickstart your part-time business so you start earning quicker."

- "I don't have to sell you on getting this wrinkle preventer as everyone wants to stop their wrinkles. But, I can help you with some extra wrinkle prevention ideas to go with your new wrinkle preventer machine."

Could we make this even easier?

Pete Andrew, the famous DJ from London, doesn't waste time. He sells coffee that helps people lose weight.

Some examples of his opening sentences to get quick "yes" decisions?

- "If you knew absolutely for certain, that drinking one coffee a day could help you and others slim down, you'd get involved wouldn't you?"
- "I am just curious. If you knew absolutely for certain, that by just recommending our healthy coffee you could make an extra £500 a month, you'd get involved wouldn't you?"

When Pete adds "absolutely certain" to his sentences, it helps him get more "yes" responses from his prospects. Pete then replies, "Then we should talk."

Let our prospects convince themselves.

We listen. We hear our prospects' problems. Now, what would be a high-level way to respond?

"You know, it is okay to keep our problems and live with them."

We create rapport. We agreed with our prospects. But how might they respond?

Most prospects will conform to the "principle of reaction." They will disagree with what we said. Expect a reply something like this:

"No. It is not okay to keep this problem. I need to fix this problem now."

We listen quietly and allow our prospects to sell themselves.

We want our prospects to make an instant "yes" decision. How?

By making it easy for them to move forward and take action.

Using good words early in our conversations will put our prospects on our side.

This all sounds good, but can I sell with integrity?

One answer is: "Respect."

Many new networkers get a twisted view of selling.

Humiliate prospects. Use high-level verbal jujitsu. Twist their words against them. Manipulate prospects against their will.

Use old-time selling techniques from 50 years ago. Gag-inducing closes. Oh my! Used car salesmen would blush. Closes such as:

- "So what is it going to take to get. You into this automobile today?"
- "Any three-year-old can see this is a good opportunity. Do I need to spell it out to you?"
- "Only fools would pass up an offer like this."
- "Do you want to pay by cash or check?"

Ugly. Abrasive. No wonder prospects reject salespeople. They deserve it. This is not the path to a fun career. Too many salespeople look at their prospects as their enemies. This sets up unneeded barriers between the salespeople and the prospects.

We don't need thick skin and a bullet-proof attitude. All we need to do is be polite. Yes, treat prospects the way we want to be treated.

Here is a better way to sell our products, services, and ideas to others. Ready?

Step #1. Listen to our prospects to see if they have a problem.

Step #2. Ask our prospects if they want to fix their problem.

Step #3. Find out when our prospects want to fix their problem. Now, or sometime in the future?

Step #4. If our prospects want to fix their problems now, we give them the option of what we offer, or allow them to continue keeping their life the same.

Polite. Social. And rejection-free. Now we can talk with prospects without the fear of becoming a sleazy, over-caffeinated, selfish salesman.

Does this feel like a better way to conduct our business?

Let's look at these steps now.

Step #1:
Listen to our prospects to see if they have a problem.

The most challenging step. Listening is a hard skill to master. Most network marketers default to talking, presenting, and showing. It is all about them and their business. Not about their prospects and their problems.

Let's think about it. Do our prospects care about us? Care about our business? No.

Our prospects are laser-focused on themselves. Prospects think about themselves and their problems 24-hours a day. Is this selfish? Yes. But that is our basic human program. Be selfish. Think about ourselves and our problems. Survive.

And some good news?

Introverts rock!

Introverts have a huge advantage in network marketing. Their superpower?

Introverts love to listen.

Extroverts are so busy talking AT prospects, that they never stop to listen to their prospects' problems. How can we solve our prospects' problems if we don't even know what problems they have?

Feel shy? Don't know what to say? Don't worry. Network marketing is so comfortable for listeners. And as a bonus, prospects love listeners.

What motivates humans the most?

Problems or rewards?

The answer is: "Problems."

Our survival program looks out for anything that threatens our well-being. We will do more to fix our problems and survive than we will to improve our lives. Yes, we want better things in life, but not as much as we want to fix our problems.

Think about hunger. When we are starving, we take action to find food. That is solving a problem. When we are not hungry, our desire to find some fine dining isn't as strong of a motivation.

If our prospects' problems are big enough, they will search out and take action immediately. We won't have to be highly skilled to help them.

All we have to do is:

A. Get our prospects to talk. Easy. People love to talk about themselves.

B. Humans love to complain about their suffering. This program comes as standard equipment in our human minds. We should make mental notes of the problems our prospects tell us. Certainly, our business could be a solution to some of their problems.

But none of this happens if we are talking. None of this happens if we are showing videos or PowerPoint presentations. The secret is to listen while our prospects talk.

Need a little problem-prompting language? Here are some ideas.

- "What are your two biggest health problems?"
- "Do you have to pay your own mobile phone bills?"
- "Did you get a utility hike last month also?"
- "Think the city will build more freeways to make our commuting easier?"
- "Does your workplace offer flexible hours yet?"
- "What does your company plan for pay raises this year?"
- "What are your two biggest skincare challenges?"

Don't worry. Prospects will pick up the conversation from here and start their litany of complaints. Need even more questions to uncover the deeper issues with our prospects' problems? Try these.

- "What do you hate the most about this problem?"
- "Is this problem frustrating?"
- "Does this problem feel embarrassing?"
- "How angry does this make you?"
- "Does this problem cause you other problems?"

Our prospects enter into a trance. Their entire thoughts are about their problems.

Want to make this even easier?

We can "up the motivation" of our prospects to fix their problems. How? By asking them to describe their problems in more detail.

The more our prospects talk about their problems, the more internal motivation they will have to fix those problems.

But what if our prospects feel little emotion or need to fix their problem? What could we do then? Let's prompt our prospects to complain more about their problem. The more they think and talk about their problem, the more urgency they feel to fix the problem. What words can we say?

Start with, "And then what happened?"

This shows our prospects that we are listening. This gives prospects a rare feeling of satisfaction. Humans love it when others listen to them.

These four words will deepen our rapport. Then, when it is our turn to talk, our prospects won't be as skeptical and judgmental.

Here are more prompting phrases we can use when they describe their problems:

- "And then what happened?"
- "How did that feel?"
- "Oh really?"
- "That is interesting."
- "That must be upsetting."
- "That sounds painful."
- "What do you think caused this?"
- "Tell me more."
- "Yes, and …?"
- "Uh-huh. I see."

Or if we can't remember any of these phrases, we can get our prospects to confirm their problems by saying, "So you have this problem, right?" This helps us know if we accurately found our prospects' problems.

Decisions come from emotion, not logic. That is why problem-solving works so well. People have emotions about their problems. A lot of emotions.

We want our prospects to think, "This person understands my problem. This person knows what I am going through."

Our rapport will be so strong with our prospects that we will find the next steps effortless. Let's continue.

Step #2:
Ask our prospects if they want to fix their problem.

Brace ourselves. Many prospects have an addiction to their suffering. Sometimes their problems provide them an identity. For example, some will describe themselves like this. "I am a diabetic." They don't say they have the problem of diabetes. Instead, it becomes how they see themselves.

The prospects who identify with their problems don't want their problems to go away. They don't want to lose their identity. Accept this.

The good news is that most people want to fix their problems. They hate that nagging feeling of depression or doom that their problems bring. These are the people we can help.

How can we ask prospects if they want to fix their problems? Easy.

Ask, "Do you want to fix your problem?" Pretty direct, but still appropriate in many situations.

A more polite version of this question? "Would it be okay if you could fix your problem?"

Want an even more tactful version? We could ask, "Have you ever considered doing something about this problem?" And then listen for their answers.

Or we could ask, "What have you tried so far?"

Remember, if our prospects have a full list of excuses why they won't or can't fix their problems, leave them alone. Don't ruin their happiness!

Our mission is to serve those prospects who want our help.

Excuses?

Yes, we can expect excuses. Many people don't want change. Change feels stressful to them. Keeping things the same, even if uncomfortable, is their preferred route in life. They will think of creative reasons why they must avoid change. Some examples.

- "I never make snap decisions. I think everything over for a minimum of three days." (How do they make their decisions when to visit the toilet?)

- "Nothing works for me. I will only find disappointment if I try." (We could counsel them for years to change their viewpoint on life. But think of all the good prospects we would miss while doing their counseling sessions. Plus, we don't want to put psychologists out of work by taking their counseling clients.)

- "I am not a salesman. I don't want to talk to my friends. I don't want to talk to strangers. I don't want to do anything!" (We should take a deep breath. Then, slowly back away.)

If we choose, we can increase our prospects' frustration with their problem by asking, "So, do you have a plan for fixing your problem?" This is a good way to see if our prospects want to change.

The reality?

Most prospects don't have a plan. Now they feel even more upset about their problem.

Yet, for many people, living in low levels of continuous pain is preferable to the stress of making a change in their lives. This is their choice, not our choice. We should respect this.

And this fear of change? Is this normal? Yes.

Humans avoid change. We don't like risk. Staying in our current situation feels safer, even if we don't like where we are. If we talk to someone who clings to their current situation, refusing change, let's allow them to live their lives. We don't have to force our agenda onto them.

Remember, our mission is to add one more option for their lives. It is up to them to take the option, or continue where they are.

How many of our prospects will truly want to fix their problems? We don't know until we ask. And, we should ask. Why?

Because we care. If they are looking for a solution, we shouldn't withhold our solution from them. They deserve a chance to ask for an option to fix their problems.

Step #3:
Find out when our prospects want to fix their problem.

Do they want to fix their problems now, or sometime in the future?

Timing is everything. If our prospect receives a government tax audit notice one minute before our conversation, what will dominate our prospect's mind? The tax audit notice.

If our prospect is getting married this afternoon, this evening's business presentation won't be the priority.

Think about our lives. Was every moment of every day the perfect time for us to join our business? No. Some mornings we feel grumpy. After a big meal, we feel no motivation. And when the dry cleaner ruins our favorite shirt, we are not in the mood for anything positive.

Is it possible to want something, but not at this very moment? Consider these two examples.

We finish a huge meal. Our friend then tells us about a gourmet steak house that just opened. We don't want to eat at this moment, but yes, we will want to go to the gourmet steak house a few hours later when we are hungry again.

Or, do we feel like taking action at 2 am in the morning? No. Bad timing.

What kind of life events make timing inconvenient? Here are a few.

- Bad news at work.
- A big promotion at work.
- A fight or disagreement at work.
- Job transfer.
- Family vacation.
- Move to a new house.
- A new baby.
- Our mother-in-law comes to visit.
- Our neighbor's cat becomes rabid.
- The school calls us about our children.
- Tonight is the last show in our favorite series.
- Christmas.
- Our television breaks down.
- Someone wrecks our car.
- The dog runs away.
- Our doctor tells us bad news.
- Newly discovered forgotten episodes of "Friends."
- Zombie apocalypse.
- Kids get chickenpox.
- Pizza delivery at the front door.
- Our lottery ticket wins.
- A new ice cream flavor is invented!

If our prospects don't want to fix their problems at this moment, it doesn't mean they don't want to fix their problems. It could be the timing. Of course, our agenda is now. But this is about our prospects and their lives, not our agenda.

How long is too long to wait? A few years back I received a phone call. The young man said, "I am ready to join." I talked to this young man briefly three years earlier. I forgot. He didn't. When his timing was right, he still remembered my message.

Don't give up on people when the timing isn't right for them. Wes Linden finishes his conversations with prospects with this message. "Is it okay if we keep in touch from time to time to see how you are doing? And I can let you know how I am doing also." This gives him permission for future follow-up. And now prospects have the chance to take action in the future when the time is right for them.

We ask our prospects to make a big change in the direction of their lives. If this very instant isn't the best time to make the change, it is okay. It is their lives, not ours. We must respect that.

But, can I help my prospects decide a bit quicker?

Sure. Early in our conversation, we can direct our prospects to consider their current situation. Some examples of these questions?

- Am I okay with doing nothing and keeping my circumstances the same?

- What will happen if I don't start earning extra money soon?

- To start my own business, how much do I think it would cost?

- Do I want a part-time business or not?
- Am I ready to start a business, or am I fooling myself and just putting off starting.
- What are the consequences if I don't do anything?
- Would I want special training to have a faster start?
- Am I afraid of a sales business?
- How many options do I have now?
- Do I want more options?
- Is now the time for me to take action, or not?
- Do I have enough money to start a part-time business ... or am I limited to a part-time job?
- Do I want to take orders from a second boss, or would I prefer to be my own boss this time?
- How much time can I put into my part-time business?
- How much risk am I willing to take with my family's money?
- Am I too old to learn something new?
- I already use 24-hours every day. What am I willing to give up to make room for a new business?
- Am I past the get-rich-quick promises I see on social media?

When our prospects slow down and think about their current situation, many will pick "now" as the best time to move forward and change their lives.

Step #4:
Gift an option.

What happens if our prospects want to fix their problem now?

We give them the option of what we offer, or allow them to continue keeping their life the same.

That is closing. Getting the decision.

Scary?

Not at all. We don't have an agenda. It is not about us.

- We gift an option to our prospects.
- It is their lives. Their decisions. Not ours.
- We are only the messenger that delivers one more option for their lives.
- They choose to take advantage of our option, or not.

And the only reason we gift this option to them now is because prospects:

1. Have a problem.
2. Want to fix their problem.
3. Want to fix their problem now.

Closing, or getting the final decision, feels like the correct next step. But how do we ask or get that decision, without pressuring our prospects or risking rejection? The answer is one word:

Options!

What does that word mean to prospects? "I am in control. I get to choose. No one will pressure me."

And what does that word mean to us? "I gift prospects an option. My duty is complete. Now it is up to them to volunteer and take action, or not. They know and can choose what is best for them at this moment in their lives."

We love options.

Prospects love options. And, the only way options can benefit our prospects is if they take advantage of the options. This is a win-win for everyone.

Imagine this scenario. At a fast-food burger restaurant, we place our order for the mega-burger with extra cheese. The order taker asks us, "Do you want fries with that?"

This is an option. Not a command. And if we don't order extra fries, the order taker will still be okay. No suicide drama, no depression, no shock. It is only an option. And how do we feel?

We appreciate that option. Who knows? We could have forgotten our addiction to extra salty fries in the excitement of ordering our mega-burger with extra cheese.

Want to be happy?

Instead of seeing our network marketing business as trying to convince prospects against their will, look at our business as gifting options to help people solve their problems. This mindset brings fun into our everyday conversations.

So how do we convince people to join our network marketing company? How do we persuade people to try network marketing?

Why not look at the situation this way:

1. Everyone already does network marketing every day.

2. Network marketing is simply recommending and promoting what we like.

3. We give people a choice. To get paid for what they are doing ... or to continue doing it for free.

We simply take the volunteers who say, "Well, as long as I am doing network marketing anyway, I might as well get paid for it."

Friends don't withhold options from friends. Everyone deserves to know their options. Then they can decide what is best for them.

Turning conversations into fun.

- Scared of talking to people? That is how I started.

- Feeling stressed when prospects treat us like evil salesmen? I can relate.

- Don't know what to say next? We all start untrained.

- Need some "happy shortcuts" that are rejection-free? Let's do it!

When we start network marketing, the skilled, successful leaders tell us, "Just talk to people!" Well, we know how that can end. Rejection. Embarrassment. Bad impressions. Broken relationships. Getting banned from weddings and funerals. Ugh!

The best way to get comfortable with talking to people is by creating some simple automatic habits. Specifically, we want to learn and practice mini-phrases that make us look like public relations geniuses. The good news is if we practice these mini-phrases long enough, they become a natural way of speaking for the rest of our lives. We won't have to remember these words. These mini-phrases will become part of us.

Let's start small with this proven phrase.

"What is new with you?" (5 words)

People love us when we ask this question. They get to talk about their favorite subject … themselves. Instant rapport. As we know, if we have rapport, the rest of our conversation gets easy. Rapport is the most important skill when talking with potential prospects.

Here are the huge instant benefits of asking, "What is new with you?"

1. Humans are interested in themselves. They think about themselves all the time. They love to talk about themselves. They can't wait for us to finish talking, so they can talk more about themselves. Our prospects love talking about themselves.

2. When prospects answer, we listen. There is no pressure on us to come up with witty conversation. And how do prospects feel about listeners? The love listeners! All we have to do is nod from time to time. Let our prospects take the spotlight and talk, talk, and talk some more. There was a survey years back. Salesmen who talked for 55 minutes, and listened for 5 minutes, got the worst results. Salesman who listened for 55 minutes, and talked for only 5 minutes were the superstars. Lesson learned.

3. Humans are programmed to complain. They want to tell us their problems. We should take note. Many of their problems could be solved by our products, services, and opportunity. This is a refreshing way to start conversations about our business solutions.

Don't believe humans are programmed to complain? Try this little test.

Go to a party. Meet new people. These "strangers" tend to complain about how the world isn't fair to them, how much they suffer, and all the bad things that happened to them recently. Why do they do this? So that we will feel sorry for them and love them more. Everyone has this program. Some have this program more than others.

And then can use the four-step process we learned earlier.

Remember?

Step #1: Listen to our prospects to see if they have a problem.

Step #2. Ask our prospects if they want to fix their problem.

Step #3. Find out when our prospects want to fix their problem. Now, or sometime in the future?

Step #4. If our prospects want to fix their now, we give them the option of what we offer, or allow them to continue keeping their life the same.

Done. Over. Finished. Our prospects then make a "yes" or "no" decision.

Closing is stress-free and rejection-free with this method. And the sale is done. Now all we have to do is explain a few details to our pre-sold, pre-closed prospects. We are both "sitting on the same side of the table." No more selling.

The problem
with goals.

Goals make us happy, right? Uh … maybe.

The reality?

Most goals torture us and make our lives miserable. What???

Imagine this scenario.

We are out of shape, eat pizza three times a day, and have a frequent eater's card at the local donut shop. The last exercise we did was pushing ourselves away from the local all-you-can-eat buffet. Our neck scarf dangles from our multiple chins.

While drinking too much beer on New Year's Eve, we make the fatal mistake. We set a goal to get in shape. Yes, we will change our lives and humiliate our critics.

How do we feel?

Awesome! Incredible! On top of the world!

We will go for our goals. Why? Because someone told us goals bring happiness into our lives. We want to be happy, right?

And then …

We wake up late on New Year's Day, levitating on our happiness high. But deep down inside, we don't want to endure the pain of exercise. Yet, we show up to the local gym, hit the weights, break a sweat, and eat a protein bar.

While on our adrenaline high, we order designer workout clothes online, and a high-tech gadget to track our expected progress.

The next morning?

Hunger pains. Muscle pains. It even hurts to smile. This is not going well.

We wonder, "How painful will it be to crawl out of this bed and get to the refrigerator for some food? Will we pass out? Could we make it? Will attempting to move out of bed trigger a heart attack? Should we call a doctor?"

January 2 brings misery.

January 3 brings more misery.

Every day in January brings more grief and pain as we drag our bodies to the gym. Our fat cells scream from the torture.

Shouldn't working for our goals make us happy?

We continue our misery, doing what we hate, every day for the year. Finally, one year later we stand in front of the mirror. We transformed our bodies. We hated every day of the past year, but … now we will take that selfie picture we dreamed about. We post our pictures on social media and announce to the world, "We did it!"

Happiness! The thrill of victory. And a good dose of "I told you so" emotion surges inside our new, fit bodies. And then …

The victory is over.

1. Now what?

2. We experienced a great day when we set our goal.

3. We loved the final day when we reached our goal.

4. And we hated the 363 days in between our two great days!

Most goals torture us like this.

A great first day. Long periods of suffering, doing stuff we hate. A victory day. And then the empty feeling as we ask ourselves, "Now what?"

The math?

Our goal gave us two days of pleasure, and 363 days of pain and unhappiness.

What else could go wrong with well-meaning goal-setting?

Imagine we set a one-year goal.

Every day during the year our subconscious mind says, "We are not there yet." We live the entire year in pre-success mode, constantly reminding and reinforcing that we are not successful at the moment. We won't feel successful until we finally cross the finish line 365 days later.

And then that feeling of success only stays a moment. We immediately go into, "Now what?"

We can set goals for our network marketing business the same way. Great visionary goal. Long days and months of doing activities we hate. Then our victory lap. And finally, the letdown.

That doesn't sound like a fun career, does it?

Instead, let's think of our Wealth/Happiness formula. What would be a better way to design the life we want?

First, let's look at the 363 days of misery. Why are we doing something we don't enjoy? Instead, how about this philosophy?

- Discover the activity we love to do.
- Then, decide where that activity can take us?
- Make that destination our new goal.

An example?

Al Cash. Yes, that was his name. Early in my career, I sponsored Al. He was a car salesman, divorced, and spent long days in the car dealership cold calling strangers to come in to see their new cars.

Al had no social life. Six days a week of long hours of phone rejection. Underpaid and miserable.

What brought joy to Al's life? Social interaction. Shaking hands. Hugs. Parties. Fun times meeting new people and creating new friends. Maybe even a chance to meet a potential spouse.

Sitting at his cubicle desk, making cold calls, and getting consistent rejection brought Al misery every day.

What activity would Al want to wake up to every morning?

Any activity that involved people. Face-to-face interaction with real people. Creating a new connection. Turning a stranger into an acquaintance and then into a friend.

So guess what?

Network marketing was made for Al.

Even if Al never earned a bonus check, he would still love to be out in the public, interacting with new people. That activity became Al's goal. Reaching out to at least one new person a day was his daily activity. He loved it. Couldn't get enough of this activity.

So what did Al do? He reached out to four or five people every day. Not for an in-your-face prospecting sales pitch, but to make a new friend.

Al didn't have to wait one year to build his business to be happy. He could be happy right now, while working towards his full-time network marketing career.

What happened? Al became one of my first leaders. Many of his new friends wanted to join him in his side business. They loved being with the outgoing, always happy car salesman who enjoyed every new connection.

Al looked at what he wanted. He decided he loved reaching out to new people daily. Then, in sort of a reverse way, Al thought, "Hey. If I meet new people every day, at the end of one year I will have many friends. Enough friends that some will want to join me in my part-time business. I will be a leader in my part-time network marketing business in one year. Then, I can quit my boring job, and live 24 hours a day doing what I love!"

Yes, Al's goal was to be a leader in one year.

The difference?

Al wouldn't suffer 363 days of mind-numbing misery. Instead, every day, starting today, brought happiness. Al lived his happiness dream to meet new people. His bonus was that he got paid for doing what he loved.

But aren't goals okay?

Yes, goals are great. But if happiness is our definition of wealth, let's re-think how we construct our goals.

Question #1: "What do I love doing?"

Question #2: "How can I make this an activity in my business?"

Question #3: "If I do this fun activity every day, what will my result be in the future?"

Think of it this way. Let's make the fun activity we enjoy ... our goal. This way we will be happy every day.

Why set activities we hate? That is a recipe for quitting. Let's put the odds in our favor and choose daily activities that won't need iron-fisted willpower.

Wealth is the time freedom to do what we want, and to enjoy ourselves during this "freedom time."

How will we feel with this new approach? Awesome.

Need some examples?

Think of gym workout enthusiasts. Every day is a fun day for them. They look forward to pushing their muscles to exhaustion, sweating rivers while straining and groaning, and loving every moment. They love the camaraderie of other workout enthusiasts. They don't put their happiness on hold. They live happiness today. They don't wait for some far-off date to celebrate their muscle growth. Today is their day.

For us? If we dread words such as exercise and gym, every day would be torture for us. To set a goal to build muscle and get into shape would be designing a life of torture. This wouldn't be a goal for us.

Or how about fishing? If someone loves fishing, it isn't about winning a fishing trophy at the annual event. Happiness is a fun weekend outdoors or talking about that secret fishing hole. Many fishermen can enjoy a day of fishing and never catch a single fish!

Goals are great.

But let's try making our goals fun to do. Every day can now be a celebration, not a living hell.

Think of goals as we would a road map. Our goal is the final destination. It gives us the direction to go. If we enjoy the drive, it doesn't matter how fast we go. We experience happiness every moment of our journey.

If we don't enjoy the journey, we will be like children in the backseat of a car who whine, "Are we there yet?" They insist on being unhappy until they arrive at the final destination.

Goals should point us in the direction we want to go while we have fun on our journey. The journey takes the longest time, so let's enjoy that part.

Think of goals this way. Our goal is to live to be 100 years old. But, we don't want to get there right away. We want to enjoy the journey.

Our network marketing business should be fun.

Why "in the moment" counts.

"Okay, kids. Stop playing with your new Christmas presents. Pose with mommy and daddy. Now, put a shocked and surprised look on your face. Wait. Make it a little happier. And Kevin, need you to close your eyes for variety. Heather, lift one arm higher. One moment, let me adjust the lighting ..."

Do kids love this? No!

We put their joy of opening presents on hold. Parents want to catch these memories, or at least catch the posed memories. Sort of ruins the celebration.

Ah, but maybe others will see their joy when these pictures show up on social media. Will they? No. People scroll fast for the next dopamine hit.

Many people have 10,000+ pictures and memories. More digital memories than they will ever review. How about those six different filter and lighting backgrounds of this scene? How many special moments and experiences did they miss because they were too busy trying to digitally capture the moment?

Holidays? Special vacations? Do we enjoy our planned time off, or are we too busy taking pictures and videos, hoping we can relive and enjoy it later? Maybe we will add these new videos to the hundreds of other videos we will never watch again.

What if we could simply enjoy what we do, instead of posing for the approval of others? What if "the moment" was our goal?

"I am a people person."

Our friend, Craig, hated observing life on a computer or phone screen. Moving pixels from one side of the screen to another was misery. Scrolling social media to watch others living their lives meant he was missing out.

Craig didn't want to live his life doing unpleasant tasks, hoping for a future payoff. Instead, Craig wanted to live now doing what he loved, in-person networking.

First, he started attending local live networking events. He loved to talk marketing with the other entrepreneurs.

Second, Craig started his own breakfast club networking group. Every Tuesday morning the group met for breakfast, exchanged leads, and got advice from Craig and others on how to market better. Craig couldn't wait to get out of bed on Tuesday mornings.

Third, Craig started his own Thursday morning breakfast club. The Tuesday morning events were already filled to capacity. Now Craig enjoyed two days a week of total bliss.

Fourth, Craig began a new habit. Every day, to everyone he met, he asked if they wanted more leads or more business. What a fun conversation. When we love our activities and habits, we have success and wealth. We get to do exactly what we want with our time.

Fifth, the customers kept rolling in. The breakfast club members kept volunteering more pre-sold customers for Craig. He could barely keep up with the new business.

For Craig, network marketing became fun. He engaged in his passion every day of the week. His passion and habits created winning days.

But is Craig's dream method of business-building our preferred method?

Maybe. Maybe not.

The lesson is that we should be like Craig.

Find the business-building method that brings us joy. With only one life to live, let's enjoy every day of our journey.

It is the journey, not the final destination that brings happiness. We must enjoy the journey.

Don't wait until 5pm on Friday to be happy.

Why the piranhas didn't eat Big Al.

I am in the Amazon with friends. Hot, humid, and uncomfortable. No breeze. Everyone is sweating. The solution?

I said, "Let's take a quick swim here in the Amazon. Something we can tell everyone back home."

Their faces turn pale. Their eyes dilate. I don't think they had the energy to respond. So as they stood there in a lifeless pool of sweat, I jumped into the river.

A couple of gasps. Someone yelled, "Get out!" More panic among the group. "The piranhas will eat you!"

Oh. So that was their concern. No wonder the frenzy.

But their fears never materialized. The piranhas scattered in fear after my "cannonball" river entry. I didn't worry at all.

This is the confidence that comes with a little knowledge. We don't have to be an expert to overcome our fears. We only have to know enough to be confident. Since I read books, I knew a bit about piranha behavior and wasn't worried. So why didn't the piranhas eat me?

1. It wasn't the dry season. Lots of water and plenty of food. There were no starving piranhas.

2. I jumped into a river, not an isolated little pond with trapped, starving piranhas.

3. I wasn't bleeding like in the movies. I refused to cut my wrists before diving in.

4. Piranhas prefer smaller prey. I was huge.

5. Piranhas love eating fish and cayman tails. They have their favorite food. Plus, I smelled from the hot, humid day.

6. Piranhas are healthy. They don't eat overweight tourists filled with saturated pizza fat. They prefer eating lean protein from fish who exercise. Piranhas religiously attend their nutrition classes.

And ... I noticed that the local village children played in the river a hundred meters away. So based upon this knowledge, my fear of becoming a piranha meal disappeared.

And then ... I was attacked by an African crocodile. Just kidding. Wrong continent.

"Fear of the unknown."

One of the many sources of fear is lack of knowledge. Our survival program paralyzes us from moving forward in the face of fear. And like my group of Amazon tourists, network marketers let their "fear of the unknown" keep them from talking to prospects.

What are their fears?

- "I don't know what to say."
- "What if they don't like me?"
- "Won't I be rejected?"
- "They will think I am a sleazy salesman."

- "I don't want my friends to think I am trying to make money off of them."
- "What if this prospect asks a question I can't answer?"
- "How will I know where to start?"

If we have fears, a little bit of knowledge can help.

What fears make our lives miserable?

- Fear of asking our boss for a raise.
- Fear of asking someone we like for a date.
- Fear of looking foolish on the dance floor.
- Fear that success will change us for the worse.
- Fear that others will think less of us.
- Fear that we will fail if our goals are too high.
- Fear of speaking in public.

And if we are like most people, we have a lot of these fears. But, we don't have to live with these fears. We don't have to allow these fears to ruin our lives. We can do something about it.

When I started network marketing, I feared speaking in public. At an early meeting, the speaker summoned me to the front of the room and asked me to introduce myself. My face turned bright red. My lips moved. No sounds came out. Failure on steroids.

The leader points out, "If you are going to become a network marketing leader, you will have to learn to speak in public and to strangers. Now is a good time to learn."

I paid half a month's salary to take a public speaking course. And then, I retook the course. What happened?

After finishing the course the second time, I was able to speak in public. Was I nervous? Yes. But no more trauma. I no longer sat in meetings with the constant fear that someone might ask me to say something.

Was it worth it? Yes! Eventually, I started to enjoy public speaking. Fears dissipate with knowledge and practice.

But what about my dancing?

Okay. I still have that fear. My rare attempts at dancing look like an amphetamine-crazed, drunk engineer, trying to do mental calculus while fighting off a swarm of mosquitos. Not pretty.

Have I learned anything new about my dancing to remove my fear of embarrassment? No. And as of now, I don't dance. Onlookers cheer my decision to avoid the dance floor.

The point is this. Fears hold us back. They make our journey miserable. But we have the power to overcome our fears with knowledge.

So what should we do?

Look at any part of our network marketing business that gives us stress and fear. Tell ourselves, "I can overcome this. I can learn to do this part of my business within my comfort zone. I can make every part of my journey a pleasurable experience."

For example, what if we had this fear?

"I am afraid to ask for an appointment?"

Why would we have this fear? Easy. If we asked for appointments, always got rejected, it would be easy to add this to our list of fears. So what could we learn to overcome this fear?

1. Read and learn how to get appointments.

What we are using now isn't working. Yet others get appointments. What do they say or do that works? Keith and I wrote the book, "How to Get Appointments Without Rejection." But, there are many other good books on how to get appointments. Why live in fear when a bit of knowledge can remove our stress?

2. Learn techniques so that prospects ask us for appointments.

If we are afraid to ask, then why not let our prospects do the asking? We would feel better about that. For example, we could use a simple curiosity hook opening, such as:

"My neighbor doesn't commute anymore. Works from home only a couple of hours a day. Would you like to know how he does it?"

If our prospects want to know more, they will ask us. We can tell them now or set an appointment for later when it is more convenient.

We don't have to live under the dark cloud of rejection. Instead, we learn how to work around this fear.

3. Change our mindset or perspective.

Are we talking ourselves into fear? We can stop that.

Imagine our current perspective is this. "I have an agenda. I want to get an appointment, sell this prospect, and build my business. If this prospect doesn't join, I will be defeated. Rejected. This feels so bad."

Yikes! The worst part is that we chose this perspective.

Instead, how about this way of looking at getting an appointment. "I have a great solution to my prospect's problems. My prospect can decide to listen to this option, or not. I only offer an option for my prospect. I don't know my prospect's current situation. I will let my prospect decide."

No more rejection. No more bad feelings. In fact, we feel obligated to give our prospect a chance to listen to our solution. Why? Because we don't want to feel bad because we withheld a possible solution that could help our prospect.

When our emotion to help prospects is greater than our fear of approaching prospects, magic happens. Approaching prospects with our option feels great. We will say to ourselves, "I care more about helping you than I care about my fear of approaching you."

Fear protects us from doing stupid stuff.

There is a place for fear. But if fear stands in our way of happiness and success, let's learn how to defeat this fear monster. Let's learn a solution within our comfort zone. We don't have to be a superhero. We only have to learn a solution.

"How to be #1 ... in Fifth-grade."

In fifth-grade, I was the #1 student in my class.

You laugh. You think, "How is that possible?"

It was easy.

All I had to do was to … show up!

I went to a one-room rural schoolhouse in Nebraska. No running water. All nine grades in one room with a teacher with uh … limited credentials. The school was basic. We did have a small bookcase and a set of 35-year-old encyclopedias. They only covered the first World War.

Now, here is the secret.

All I had to do was to show up as I was the only student in fifth-grade. I rocked! (I was the only student in sixth-grade also, but that is another story.)

"Showing up" is the same in our network marketing career. If we show up enough times, we put the odds of success in our favor. We can only be lucky if we are still in the game.

Here is what happened when I started my network marketing career.

Nothing.

I kept showing up, but I didn't get any results. Now, I am not an idiot. After all, I was #1 in my fifth-grade class. I noticed that other people did get results. And I wondered why? It turned out that they knew how to talk to people better.

Okay. Now I had a decision to make.

Do I learn what to say? Or do I go back to my friends who didn't join and say, "You were right. I will never be successful at this."

I gambled and took a chance. I took a course on how to talk to people. I read books. And I attended more trainings.

Now when I showed up, prospects joined.

Yes, I figured this all out on my own. But you would expect that from the valedictorian of the 5th class, wouldn't you?

Two lessons.

Lesson #1: At the very minimum, we have to show up.

Lesson #2: If we show up and don't get results, it is time for us to improve our skills.

Seems easy, but why don't we do this?

Because we are not comfortable with how we build our businesses. Our brains don't want us to feel bad, get rejected, and feel uncomfortable. Our brains hate pain and love feeling great.

So instead of fighting our brains, let's create activities we love that naturally build our businesses. Some examples of how others found "their way" to build?

- Bring cookies to the PTA meetings. Talk to the smiling cookie-eaters.

- Start a local walking club that attracts prospects looking to be healthy.

- Arrange a community fashion show that features our skincare and cosmetics.

- Teach an investing class.

- Arrange a local small business expo.

- Daily tips posted on social media.

- Offer samples of what we sell.

If prospecting is fun, we will never stop.

We don't need extra motivation to have fun.

Personal development?

Tony blushed, "My mind is my biggest enemy. It works full-time to sabotage and kill my momentum. I believed my teachers who told me that I was a slacker. I believed my friends who told me to be happy where I am. I let my negative environment become my reality."

Tony's goal?

To feel good about himself. His network marketing career suffered a bad pattern. Build a little. Get mad at his sponsor. Quit. Start again with another company. Get mad at the company. Quit. Repeat this process again and again.

Tony realized the cause of his continuing disasters was his perspective and attitude. He knew the world wouldn't change for him. We wish the world would change to our whims and wishes, but alas, it is not to be.

Instead, Tony knew he had to change. But when we start from zero, the first step should be a baby step. We need momentum.

Tony's plan?

To do something that made him happy. Something easy. Something where success was completely within his control. And something where he wouldn't need iron-fisted motivation to do it.

His solution?

Enjoy 15 minutes a day of personal development.

He said, "I spend 23 hours and 45 minutes every day with the negative things in my life. But I will take a mental holiday for 15 minutes every day and pour positive things into my brain. I will change me."

Did it work?

Well, here is what happened.

First, Tony passively listened to 15 minutes a day of personal development. Reading seemed too hard. Start small. Make the first tiny steps easy. Build some momentum.

Next, after a few weeks, Tony began to mentally question the negative talk of his coworkers. He thought, "Wow. Their conversations are depressing. I don't like the feelings I get from these negative conversations."

Next, Tony thought, "Everyone has a mind. Even me. I might as well learn how it works. I want to be in charge." This personal development was getting to be a lot more fun. In fact, it felt better than scrolling through mindless videos on social media. Progress.

Now, let's ask ourselves these two questions.

1. "Was Tony enjoying his personal development time?"

2. "Did Tony's minutes of positivity make him feel happy?"

Yes!

So who did Tony want to associate with in the future?

Other positive thinkers of course. And that led Tony to network marketing.

Network marketers decide to change their lives. They are doers. They want to improve their circumstances and believe in possibilities. The better person we become, the more others feel attracted to us. Plus, feeling better about ourselves is a great bonus.

Now, Tony's desire for personal development made a giant leap forward. He surrounded himself with like-minded people. Our associations rub off on us. If our four best friends are drunks, chances are we will be a drinker. We want to surround ourselves with people moving forward and let their positive attitudes influence us.

Tony's personal development routine increased in time, and he expanded his interests.

His new interest? People. Specifically, people skills. Tony's new addiction was reading and listening to new ideas so that he could understand others better. His improved people skills grew his network marketing business.

The good news is that Tony loved every step along the way. He didn't do anything that felt disgusting or embarrassing. He didn't force himself to do tasks that he hated. And his prospects noticed this. They wanted the same feelings. It was easy for them to follow in Tony's footsteps.

Will personal development make a difference?

Zig Ziglar once asked his audience: "Can you do something to make your life worse in the next three weeks?"

The audience said: "Yes, of course."

Then Zig said: "Can you do something to make your life better in the next three weeks?"

Oh.

Making our lives worse is easy to visualize. But we seldom think about the inverse, making our lives better.

We have to admit that we can make a difference. This is within our control, and it is so easy to do.

If we don't like our lives, and we don't take action, our situation tends to get worse.

Our lazy brain programs beat us into submission. We accept our situation as normal. And we never grow from this point.

Wealth is happiness.

We choose what we do want with our time. That is true happiness.

Tony became wealthy even before his bigger paychecks arrived. Can we take a few lessons from Tony's happiness? How about these?

- A 15-minute habit is easy to do if we like the activity.
- Start small. If 15 minutes feels like too much, then start with 5 minutes. We want to build personal momentum.
- If we do personal development over time, we will grow and want more.
- Our goals feel more realistic as we build our minds.

Personal development?

We either commit to growing, or we commit to falling behind.

Learning something new every day keeps us young.

If we love what we do, it will never feel like work.

Can Big Al become a Mexican food spokesman?

Question: Why doesn't the "Big Taco" restaurant chain sponsor you or make you their spokesman? You seem to be their biggest fan, and a huge repeat customer.

Answer: Well, it seems they insist on a healthy, athletic body type to advertise their 730-calorie bean and cheese burrito.

I can visualize my interview now.

Big Taco: "So do you have any acting experience or credentials?"

Big Al: "Uh, no. But I have a vision board. Does that help?"

Big Taco: "No. Well, do you look fit and healthy?"

Big Al: "Uh, no. My diet has pretty much been fattening Mexican food for the past 50 years. But, I chant affirmations. Does that help?"

Big Taco: "No."

Big Al: "I believe in attraction marketing. How about that?"

Big Taco: "No. I am losing patience with you."

Big Al: "I work on my personal growth daily. What do you think?"

Big Taco: "Your personal growth must be related to your waistline's personal growth. Forget it!"

Big Al: "I can set goals. Well?"

Big Taco: "No! You are fat, out-of-shape, a picture of bad health, and have no acting experience. You don't have the skills for the job of spokesman. Get over it. But you might qualify for a drive-through order-taker. Can you put on an extra 20 pounds and mumble?"

Okay, let's face reality.

I don't have the skills to be their spokesman.

It takes more than a cheery attitude to qualify.

In network marketing, there is a balance too. We need attitude … and skills.

When we invest our time in personal development, yes, mindset is important. While mindset is the most important element, we still need skills to make our dreams come true.

If we don't have skills in our network marketing business, how can we make a difference?

Our prospects don't care about our vision board at home, our "why" … or if we chanted affirmations this morning.

What matters when we talk to prospects?

Our skills.

Our ability to get our message inside of their heads, so they can make a choice. This isn't easy when we start, but we can learn.

Having a great attitude, vision boards, and hyper-motivation is great. We just need to add skills to get the job done.

We don't want to look in the mirror and ask, "Why are my goals not working?"

Goals don't go to work. We go to work. We must learn the skills to get our message inside the heads of our prospects.

Balance.

Personal development means mindset training for most people. That is great. But we need to add skill development to make things happen. Invest part of our personal development time into learning how to build our business.

Summary.

The average day in a real network marketing pro and an amateur networker looks almost the same.

Every day the network marketing pro makes a contact or two, or maybe plants a seed, while the wannabe amateur networker spends those few minutes doing nothing.

98% of their days are identical.

The difference? The network marketing pro concentrates on happiness, making the activity fun.

One year later? The network marketing pro has a residual income and is on the way to financial freedom. The amateur networker has frustration and smaller results.

What can we do to be happy network marketers?

1. We can concentrate on ways to build our business within our comfort zones.

2. We can learn new skills so that our efforts will produce better results.

Ready to learn more skills?

Here is the next book to kickstart our happy network marketing career.

—Keith & Tom "Big Al" Schreiter

The best book ever with the fastest shortcuts?

Out of 35+ Big Al training books for network marketing, this is the best place to start.

bigalbooks.com/quickstart

Want free awesome tips to help build your network marketing business?

Great examples of exactly what to say, and exactly what to do. The best words and phrases to get results.

Join 30,000+ network marketers who look forward to these business-building ideas twice a week in their email.

Tell us where to send your twice-weekly free tips.

BigAlBooks.com/free

More from Big Al Books

See them all at BigAlBooks.com

Mindset Series

Secrets to Mastering Your Mindset
Take Control of Your Network Marketing Career

Breaking the Brain Code
Easy Lessons for Your Network Marketing Career

How to Get Motivated in 60 Seconds
The Secrets to Instant Action

Prospecting and Recruiting Series

Overcoming Objections
Making Network Marketing Rejection-Free

Hooks! The Invisible Sales Superpower
Create Network Marketing Prospects Who Want to Know More

How to Get Appointments Without Rejection
Fill Our Calendars with Network Marketing Prospects

Create Influence
10 Ways to Impress and Guide Others

How to Meet New People Guidebook
Overcome Fear and Connect Now

How to Get Your Prospect's Attention and Keep It!
Magic Phrases for Network Marketing

10 Shortcuts Into Our Prospects' Minds
Get Network Marketing Decisions Fast!

How To Prospect, Sell And Build Your Network Marketing Business With Stories

26 Instant Marketing Ideas To Build Your Network Marketing Business

51 Ways and Places to Sponsor New Distributors
Discover Hot Prospects For Your Network Marketing Business

First Sentences for Network Marketing
How To Quickly Get Prospects On Your Side

Big Al's MLM Sponsoring Magic
How To Build A Network Marketing Team Quickly

Start SuperNetworking!
5 Simple Steps to Creating Your Own Personal Networking Group

Getting Started Series

How to Build Your Network Marketing Business in 15 Minutes a Day

3 Easy Habits For Network Marketing
Automate Your MLM Success

Quick Start Guide for Network Marketing
Get Started FAST, Rejection-FREE!

Four Core Skills Series

How To Get Instant Trust, Belief, Influence and Rapport!
13 Ways To Create Open Minds By Talking To The Subconscious Mind

Ice Breakers!
How To Get Any Prospect To Beg You For A Presentation

Pre-Closing for Network Marketing
"Yes" Decisions Before The Presentation

The Two-Minute Story for Network Marketing
Create the Big-Picture Story That Sticks!

Personality Training Series (The Colors)

The Four Color Personalities for MLM
The Secret Language for Network Marketing

Mini-Scripts for the Four Color Personalities
How to Talk to our Network Marketing Prospects

Why Are My Goals Not Working?
Color Personalities for Network Marketing Success

How To Get Kids To Say Yes!
Using the Secret Four Color Languages to Get Kids to Listen

Presentation and Closing Series

Closing for Network Marketing
Getting Prospects Across The Finish Line

The One-Minute Presentation
Explain Your Network Marketing Business Like A Pro

How to Follow Up With Your Network Marketing Prospects
Turn Not Now Into Right Now!

Retail Sales for Network Marketers
How to Get New Customers for Your MLM Business

Leadership Series

The Complete Three-Book Network Marketing Leadership Series
Series includes: How To Build Network Marketing Leaders Volume
One, How To Build Network Marketing Leaders Volume Two, and
Motivation. Action. Results.

How To Build Network Marketing Leaders
Volume One: Step-By-Step Creation Of MLM Professionals

How To Build Network Marketing Leaders
Volume Two: Activities And Lessons For MLM Leaders

Motivation. Action. Results.
How Network Marketing Leaders Move Their Teams

What Smart Sponsors Do
Supercharge Our Network Marketing Team

More books...

Why You Need to Start Network Marketing
How to Remove Risk and Have a Better Life

How To Build Your Network Marketing Nutrition Business Fast

How Speakers, Trainers, and Coaches Get More Bookings
12 Ways to Flood Our Calendars with Paid Events

How To Build Your Network Marketing Utilities Business Fast

Getting "Yes" Decisions
What insurance agents and financial advisors can say to clients

Public Speaking Magic
Success and Confidence in the First 20 Seconds

Worthless Sponsor Jokes
Network Marketing Humor

About the Authors

Keith Schreiter has 30+ years of experience in network marketing and MLM. He shows network marketers how to use simple systems to build a stable and growing business.

So, do you need more prospects? Do you need your prospects to commit instead of stalling? Want to know how to engage and keep your group active? If these are the types of skills you would like to master, you will enjoy his "how-to" style.

Keith speaks and trains in the U.S., Canada, and Europe.

Tom "Big Al" Schreiter has 50+ years of experience in network marketing and MLM. As the author of the original "Big Al" training books in the late '70s, he has continued to speak in over 80 countries on using the exact words and phrases to get prospects to open up their minds and say "YES."

His passion is marketing ideas, marketing campaigns, and how to speak to the subconscious mind in simplified, practical ways. He is always looking for case studies of incredible marketing campaigns that give usable lessons.

As the author of numerous audio trainings, Tom is a favorite speaker at company conventions and regional events.